WHY DRESDEN WAS BOMBED

A Review of the Reasons and Reactions

By

Mr. Joseph F. Tustin

Chief Historian, Historical Division
Office Of Information Services
Headquarters, United States Air Forces in Europe

11 December 1954

Table of Contents

Cover photo:Dresden, after the bombing. Original caption: *Tens of thousands of deaths were stacked on the streets of Dresden in high stacks and burnt, some without identification.* Image maintained by the German Federal Archive (Deutsches Bundesarchiv).

1. - Introduction: Aspects Of The Controversy

Ever since the end of the Second World War the bombing of Dresden has been a highly controversial subject, not only among the Germans themselves, but also with the Communists in the Soviet Zone of Germany, who have capitalized upon the air raids (which in reality aided the Red Army) to further Communist propaganda and sway German sympathies away from Western influences.[1]

To be sure, the destruction of this beautiful city with such great loss of life, so late in the war, was catastrophic in the extreme for the German people, an immense misfortune of war.

The tragedy of Dresden is even more poignantly etched on the mind by the impact of the tremendous events and absolute chaos which climaxed its last days when multitudes of refugees, fleeing from the east before the onrushing Red Army, swarmed by the tens of thousands into the overcrowded city. Unending streams of refugees poured into Dresden, by day and by night, jamming all the railroad stations, blocking the streets with vehicles, filling each house to the last place, and camping by the thousands in the cold, wet weather in the city squares, parks, and the meadows by the Elbe river.[2] On the night of its destruction,

Dresden sheltered 700,000 refugees according to German estimates,[3] in addition to its normal population of over 600,000 residents.[4]

A well known German author states that "This great city sheltered 1,130,000 human beings within its walls as its destruction approached, as its hour struck."[5]

Such was the hapless predicament of Dresden, celebrated as the "German Florence,"[6] and the most beautiful city in Europe, on the night of 13-14 February 1945, now remembered by many Germans as "Die Mordnacht von Dresden."[7] This disparaging insinuation echoes the Nazi accusations of "terror bombing" by the Allies during the war. And now, almost ten years later, with war passions abated and memories fading, the revival of this old charge, albeit in different form, calls for a dispassionate review of the detailed reasons for the bombing of Dresden beyond the scant facts hitherto disclosed in American papers in Germany.

It should be pointed out here that the United States Air Forces in Europe (USAFE) is the lineal descendant of the wartime United States Strategic Air Forces in Europe (USSTAF)[8] which, along with the Bomber Command of the Royal Air Force (RAF), carried out the strategic bombing of Germany and German held Europe. Hence, it is quite likely that USAFE, as the successor to USSTAF,[9] inherited *ex post facto*, in many German minds, part of the responsibility for Dresden's destruction, although such sophistry would be completely illogical to American thinking. Nevertheless, the sins of the father are sometimes visited upon the son, regardless of legitimate justification.

Needless to state, this limited report is not an attempt to justify the bombing of Dresden but rather to record all the known historical facts which may have relation to it. Certainly, not all relevant information was available for study, particularly the specific Allied directives ordering the air attacks, or pertinent high level documents in the British Air Ministry in London and in the Departments of Defense and State in Washington, as well as any possible documentary evidence of the exact Soviet request for this particular bombing assistance.[10] However, all available sources known to the writer have been studied, both official and unofficial, as well as certain German information on the subject; extracts of these are included in this report and accompanying appendices. The reference documentation includes data from books and reports on Allied wartime plans and policies which actuated the fateful decision to bomb Dresden.

2. Events Leading to the Bombardment

Before outlining the reasons for the air attacks on Dresden it is necessary to understand something of the military situation at the time. The reader will recall that the final military objective of the Allied and Red armies was to establish a junction somewhere in eastern Germany, thus forcing the enemy to capitulate. As the war approached its climax in early 1945, most of western Germany was in Allied hands and the Red Army was within sixty miles of Dresden. The continued convergence of these armies toward that city began to shape the remaining German held territory into two rough triangles, the apex of each joining at Dresden, forming a gigantic hourglass.

Fate thus placed Dresden in the very center of the maelstrom, the last great railroad center left in Germany, through which the remaining German forces in the northern triangle could funnel down to the southern triangle and into the "National Redoubt" in the Austrian-Bavarian Alps.[11] Here, it was confidently expected by the Supreme Allied Commander, General Eisenhower, a last stand would be made by the remnants of the German Army, should they be able to retreat into these formidable and almost inaccessible mountains.[12]

In his memoirs, Sir Winston S. Churchill, the British Prime Minister, mentions only the bare fact that Dresden was bombed in February 1945. He notes, however, that the city was "then a centre of communications of Germany's Eastern Front."[13] Sir Winston also reveals that General Eisenhower's main attack was to be made in the direction of Dresden in order to truncate the German forces and prevent possible resistance in the so-called National Redoubt in the Austrian Alps. This plan was completely acceptable to Marshal Joseph Stalin and indicated mutual agreement with immediate war aims. Referring to a direct telegram that General Eisenhower sent to Marshal Stalin on 28 March 1945, Churchill states:

> Eisenhower said that after isolating the Ruhr he proposed to make his main thrust along the axis Erfurt-Leipzig-Dresden, which, by joining hands with the Russians, would cut in two the remaining German forces. A secondary advance through Regensburg to Linz, where also he expected to meet the Russians, would prevent "the consolidation of German resistance in the redoubt in Southern Germany." Stalin agreed readily. He said that the proposal "entirely coincides

with the plan of the Soviet High Command."[14]

Up to 13 February 1945, Dresden had escaped serious bombardment.[15] Previously, many great German cities had been virtually destroyed with heavy loss of civilian life, the direct result of the relentless air attacks made by the Royal Air Force and the U.S. Strategic Air Forces, based upon the long range strategic plan[16] designed to bring Nazi Germany to her knees.

At the Malta Conference on 30 January 1945 the Combined Chiefs of Staff [17] had decided to throw the combined weight of RAF and United States Army Air Forces (USAAF) heavy bombers into the battle in the East. This decision apparently anticipated a formal request for such assistance made a few days later (4 February 1945) at the Yalta Conference by the Russian General A. E. Antonov, Chief of Staff of the Red Army General Staff.[18]

At Yalta, the Western Allies and the Russians were "in strong agreement" that the strategic air forces might prevent German reinforcement of the disintegrating eastern front. This assistance was particularly designed to block the transportation centers through which the German Army might transfer units from west to east, especially the cities of

Berlin, Leipzig, Dresden, Cottbus, and Chemnitz.[19] Concerning this decision, the official history of *The Army Air Forces In World War II* has this to say:

> . . There was also a hope that heavy air raids would increase the panic and confusion already prevalent in those cities, which were thoroughly frightened by the sudden Russian advance and full of refugees. Pandemonium in Berlin, particularly, might have a decisive effect in speeding up the disintegration of Hitler's regime. Accordingly, the air leaders at Malta issued with the strong approval of General Marshall, and with what they took to be the concurrence of AAF Headquarters, a revised directive.[20] As a second priority (after synthetic oil plants) came "Berlin, Leipzig, Dresden, and associated cities where heavy attack will cause great confusion in civilian evacuation from the east and hamper reinforcements." As a third priority the heavy bombers would direct their efforts on communications in the Ruhr-Cologne-Kassel area to keep the Germans

from withdrawing forces in the west to bolster the east.[21]

The catastrophic results of these air operations so reduced the German capacity for resistance that transportation targets as far east as Cottbus and Dresden were attacked "in direct support of the Russian ground armies."[22]

After the war Sir Arthur T. Harris, Marshal of the Royal Air Force,[23] stated that he had been ordered to attack Dresden because it was considered to be "a target of the first importance for the offensive on the Eastern front."[24] By February 1945, Dresden had become the main center of communications for the defense of Germany on the southern half of the eastern front. The Supreme Allied Headquarters[25] decided that a heavy air attack on Dresden would disorganize these communications and also render the city useless as a controlling center for defense. Further, Dresden was a large center of war industry, a target of the "highest importance."[26]

Dresden, the capital of Saxony, was an important railroad center. The main railroad connections between southern and eastern Germany passed through the city, and several rail lines branched out to Leipzig and other parts of industrial Saxony. The harbor was of considerable importance to the freight traffic on the Elbe river. Dresden's transportation network included large railroad marshalling yards, freight yards with considerable storage facilities, extensive locomotive repair shops of great importance, an inland harbor, and railway maintenance shops. There were also factories of importance to the German war effort, in the Dresden area, including an iron foundry, two aircraft repair factories, as well as engineering and armament industries, chemical and explosive factories, shipbuilding yards, and flour mills. Several important factories manufactured electric motors, precision and optical instruments for submarines, and numerous light engineering products. The munitions workshops in the old arsenal occupied an extensive area to the north of Neustadt[27] on the right bank of the Elbe, in the industrial region past the aerodrome to a large heath where munitions were stored in quantities.[28]

3. - The Main Allied Attacks

All was peaceful in Dresden during the evening of 13 February 1945 until half past nine that night, when a general alarm was sounded throughout the city. The first RAF attack began forty minutes later . . . "And then came the inferno!" Graphically, a German author relates: "The clock of the Church of Our Lady showed 22.09 o'clock. Hell broke loose. The earth trembled. Bombs exploded, drowning the noise of the motors."[29]

The Royal Air Force made two assaults on Dresden on the night of 13-14 February. In the first, 244 "Lancaster" bombers formed the first wave, in the second, 529 bombers of the same type took part. In all, 2,659 tons of explosive and incendiary bombs were dropped on the city, which was then the main center of communications in the southern half of the Eastern front. Explaining the reason for these attacks, the history of the Royal Air Force states: "The destruction of these communications was part of the Anglo-American plan for the support of the Russian advance. The crews of Bomber Command very faithfully fulfilled their task … ."[30] Smoke from this terrible bombardment was still rising to 15,000 feet by the time the American bombers arrived over Dresden in daylight on 14 February to make their bombing run by instrument.[31] The heart of the city, the Old Town, and to a lesser extent the New Town across the Elbe, were engulfed by fire, an awesome scene of utter devastation.[32] Now followed 316 "Flying Fortresses" (four motor bombers), raining 782 more tons[33] of bombs down on the marshalling yards of the ruined city, adding to the already devastated area observed in the district of Johannstadt. The main marshalling yards in the Old Town were still burning: an engine roundhouse, freight station, and numerous freight cars in the heavily loaded yards. Damage was severe to public and administrative buildings, while residential damage was scattered but severe in places, as far as the suburb of Loschwitz. Other destruction observed by American pilots included the main railroad station, barracks, industrial buildings, and the "Augustus" and "Carola" bridges spanning the Elbe.[34]

A German account of the combined RAF-USSTAF attacks states that:

> After the first attack this great city was burning in an area seven kilometers long and four kilometers wide. The second attack began two and one half hours later. Thirty five minutes long the earth trembled under the impact of numberless bombs . . . . And

> ten hours later the third attack followed in daylight in undiminished intensity on the last suburbs of Dresden not yet burned.[35]

It was this combined attack that apparently caused the tumult about "terror bombing," again voiced by Nazi propaganda. In view of such serious charges and their possible morale effect throughout Germany and the rest of the world, General Marshall felt that, "The Secretary of War had to be apprised of Dresden's importance as a transportation center and the Russian request for its neutralization.[36] Even the RAF official report on the attacks went to unusual length to explain how the city had grown into a great industrial center and was therefore an important target.[37]

Six air raids in all were made on Dresden by the Eighth Air Force of the U.S. Strategic Air Forces based in England. All the attacks were made on the marshalling yards, except those of 7 October 1944 and 17 April 1945, when industrial targets were bombed. In the six American attacks the Eighth Air Force lost nineteen bombers; the losses of air crews are unavailable. A summary of bombing statistics follows:

Tons of Bombs Dropped

7 Oct 1944: 38 sorties dropped 100.5 tons of high explosive bombs and no incendiaries.
15 Jan 1945: 133 sorties dropped 279.8 tons of high explosive bombs and 41.6 tons of incendiaries.
14 Feb 1945: 316 sorties dropped 487.7 tons of high explosive bombs and 294.3 tons of incendiaries.
15 Feb 1945: 211 sorties dropped 465.6 tons of high explosive bombs and no incendiaries.
2 Mar 1945: 406 sorties dropped 940.3 tons of high explosive bombs and 140.5 tons of incendiaries.
17 Apr 1945: 572 sorties dropped 1,526.4 tons of high explosive bombs and 164.5 tons of incendiaries.

Total for all sorties: 1,676 sorties dropped 3,800.3 tons of high explosive bombs and 640.9 tons of incendiaries.

As the reader will note by the foregoing statistics, the heaviest American attack on Dresden was not made until 17 April 1945, just three weeks before the war ended. By then, the cumulative total of bombs used in the six American attacks exceeded the tonnage dropped in the RAF's two wave attack by almost forty per cent. Available German accounts of Dresden's bombing appear to point up only the main attacks of 13-15 February, but then, from their perspective, the city was already considered dead.[39] Following the February bombing, the RAF Bomber Command issued a report on the analysis of damage to Dresden, explaining: "But if casualties were exceptionally high and damage to residential areas great, it was also evident the city's industrial and transportation establishments had been blotted out."[40]

On the other hand, the wartime German Minister for Armaments and War Production, Albert Speer,[41] stated after the war that the air attacks did not completely destroy Dresden's war industry, as claimed by the Allies, and, as is now overlooked in present day German writings.

> Day attacks made in addition to night raids would only have had some effect if in the main they, like the night raids, had taken the form of incendiary attacks. Such a system of attack was employed on Dresden, and despite all previous raids throughout the Reich during the three years,
> it caused a considerable shock effect. Nevertheless, the industrial life of Dresden recovered with comparative rapidity.[42]

If Herr Speer's statement was accurate it would indicate that some war production revived in Dresden in spite of the terrible bombings, so greatly lamented today. At all events, the city actually ceased to be a military center of communications as the RAF Bomber Command claimed, a fact corroborated by Colonel General Jodl, Chief of the Joint General Staff of the German Army High Command. After the war General Jodl told American interviewers that, "Attacks on Dresden eliminated it as a railroad junction completely."[43] This end result was, after all, one of the principal objectives of the final Allied strategic air offensive.

4. - The Aftermath: Its Impact On Subsequent Events

The destruction of Dresden set off emotional waves of sorrow, fear, and anger within the shrinking German Reich; no greater damage had been done to any other German city during the war, save at Hamburg.[44]

Stunned by this disaster, Germans were also bitter to learn of the "most absurd piece" yet produced by the Nazi Propaganda Ministry. Overnight posters appeared everywhere, printed on the "well known red paper," which read:

PROCLAMATION TO THE SORELY AFFLICTED POPULATION OF DRESDEN!

> The Fuhrer knows of your suffering and your distress. Do not give yourselves up to despair, do not capitulate! The Fuhrer will avenge you. In a few days retaliation will come! Endure until the glorious victory of German history![45]

The promised "retaliation" soon became apparent: It was Hitler's expressed intention to have ten thousand Allied airmen prisoners of war shot for the air raid on Dresden.[46] Maddened also by the catastrophe, Joseph Goebbels, the Nazi Propaganda Chief, demanded the repudiation of the Geneva Convention, the massacre of forty thousand Allied airmen, and the use of two new and terrible poison gases, "Tabun" and Sarin."[47] None of these desperate threats were carried out, fortunately, since Germany was in its eleventh hour before defeat.

Conflicting claims have been made on the number of casualties resulting from the air attacks on Dresden, some greatly exaggerated and obviously untrue. Immediately following this disaster the Deputy Director of the German Propaganda Bureau sent this extravagant report to Berlin:

> The estimated number of persons killed during the attacks was 350,000 to 400,000. More than a million persons were in Dresden during this night. The original population was approximately 670,000; one third of all persons staying in the city during this night lost their lives.[48]

Another doubtful account supporting an immense death toll was printed in the Swiss journal, *Flugwehr and Technik* (Air Defense and Technique), which stated: "According to a reliable source, the total dead during the three heavy attacks was said to be 100,000." This report conjectured that only the victims among Dresden's inhabitants were counted, without taking the refugees into consideration.[49]

From the evidence presented here it is likely that the number of persons killed was considerably below 100,000, a figure also loosely quoted and accepted apparently without question by an American correspondent of *LIFE* magazine who visited Dresden earlier this year.[50]

The lowest estimate given by the Russians was 25,000, the highest 32,000 persons. But the Germans base their higher estimates on the numbers treated in improvised hospitals and first aid stations, and on the bodies cremated in the burned out railway station.[51]

One may reasonably consider that the figures given by the German authors, Herr Rumpf and Herr Gorlitz, are closer to the correct figure than the excessive death toll earlier mentioned. The former author stated that by April 1945 approximately 30,000 bodies had been recovered. Without question, a vast number of the missing and presumed dead were buried under the ruins, estimated at another 30,000 persons, making the total number of victims 60,000, the same figure mentioned by the latter authors.[52] One thing is certain: the exact toll of this tragic event will never be known and will continue to create never ending speculation and controversy.

The enormous loss of human life at Dresden has cast its shadow far outside of Germany, to British Rhodesia in Africa, where one of the architects of the attack now lives in retirement: Marshal of the RAF Sir Arthur Harris. Weighing in his conscience the military reasons vis-a-vis the moral responsibility for the bombing, the former commander of the RAF Bomber Command wrote:

> I know that the destruction of so large and splendid a city at this late stage of the war was considered unnecessary even by a good many people who admit that our earlier attacks were as fully justified as any other operation of war. Here I will only say that the attack on Dresden was at the time considered a military necessity by much more important people than myself, and that if their judgment was right the same arguments must apply that I have set out in

> an earlier chapter in which I said what I think about the ethics of bombing as a whole.[53]

On the other side of the hill, there was an almost unanimous opinion among captured German military leaders that the war could not have been won without Allied air superiority which decimated Germany's cities and industry. To quote one of the ten statements appended to this narrative, Infantry General Georg Thomas, military chief of German production, pointedly said: "Bombing alone could not have beaten Germany, but without bombing the war would have lasted for years longer."[54]

During the early summer of 1949, while the Berlin Airlift was still in operation, an American journalist made a secret fact finding journey to the Soviet Zone of Germany where he visited a number of important cities, among which was Dresden, then under Russian military rule. This was before the establishment of the so-called German Democratic Republic, the present Communist government in the Soviet Zone, and at a time when the Russians had already begun their attempts to inflame the East Germans against the United States.

Returning to Dresden after seventeen years, the journalist walked through the center of the deserted Old Town. The baroque beauty of Germany's architectural pride had vanished in seven square miles of destruction. From a ragged little girl he bought a guidebook of the few remaining historical buildings. It said that 117,000 people had once lived in this part of the town, now only 900 were left. But unexpectedly, he found a yellow page inserted at the end of the guidebook, which read;

A TIMELY APPENDIX

> At a time when the American and British air forces are hailing the Air Bridge to Berlin as a service to peace, their real face is shown by the desolation now reigning in Germany's cities. That has been done to our beautiful Dresden has been done a hundred times over from Munich to Nuremberg and from Frankfurt to Lubeck. The cultural heritage of centuries has been destroyed, the lives of defenseless women and children have perished in fire and ashes; yet the war industries had been barely touched.

> Dresden's churches, operas, and museums are gone; but Goering's air force barracks and Hitler's ammunition factories in the suburbs have passed through the war almost unharmed.
> The Soviet Union has never believed in the bombing of civilian populations and objects of historical and cultural value. Throughout the war the great Soviet air fleets have concentrated their deadly power only on tactical bombing, the destruction of the Hitlerite armies. Remember that when you stand and gaze over the desert in the heart of Dresden and when you hear the word "humanity" used by the American air adventurers in Berlin.

After reading this touching bit of Soviet sentimentality, the American journalist reflected on their new found righteous defense of cultural values, particularly since he had just recently witnessed the destruction of some ancient castles and Renaissance palaces in Saxony by these selfsame Russians.[55]

5. - Conclusion

It is clearly evident from the historical data presented in this narrative that the final stepped up air offensive of the Allies was designed to end the war as quickly as possible, even at the risk of increased civilian casualties, for there could be no hope of preventing further bloodshed to the armies of all belligerents, as well as civilians, until the fighting actually ceased. Of this there was little expectation until the German Army was finally crushed between the gigantic pincers of the Allied and Red armies, then rapidly closing on Dresden.

Yet one man alone could have spared Dresden its death throes, had he thought more of his Fatherland than of himself: Hitler, intransigent to the end, must bear some responsibility in History for the destruction of Dresden, since he wished to see his people dead and his country in ruins before he would surrender.[56]

Finis

APPENDICES

ARTICLE ON BOMBING OF DRESDEN-LIFE MAGAZINE

TAKEN FROM SPECIAL ISSUE OF THE MAGAZINE LIFE,
"GERMANY, A GIANT AWAKENED," 10 MAY 1954, PAGE 50
BOMBING U.S.S.R. SOUGHT IS TURNED AGAINST U. S.

Prewar Dresden, so beautiful it was sometimes called the Florence of the Elbe, was shattered by Allied bombers on Feb. 13, 1945, with a loss of 100,000 lives. This, Correspondent Lang discovered, is something the Communists do not permit the people of Dresden to forget. Lang cabled:

"You will find that the people of Dresden do not like Americans" the East German official who arranged our trip warned us in Berlin. He was at least partly right. What differentiates Dresden from other bombed cities in Germany, and several were bombed more heavily and more often, is the hatred cultivated in the ruins. A large sign at the entrance to the Swinger, the bombed-out court of Saxon kings, reminds tourists that the cultural damage there was caused by the English and the Americans. Visitors to Dresden are thoughtfully given a book of photographs, *The Camera Accuses*, which shows the chaos after the bombing, as well as bodies being incinerated in the streets.

"Each year on Feb. 13 the Communist authorities sponsor commemorative demonstrations to freshen up painful memories. City officials never refer to the destruction as due to the war, but in a stock phrase which even appears on postcards depicting prewar Dresden: "Destroyed by Anglo-American bombers." All this had had its effect. When Photographer Crane and I visited an old people's home we were buttonholed by an elderly woman, her head framed prettily by white hair, who angrily insisted that we go down to Altstadt, the old city, 'to photograph the destruction caused by you Americans.'

"The real reason Dresden was bombed has long since been lost on the people who live there. This became apparent in a conversation I had with a young man named Hans-Jurgen Meyer, a teacher in the Young Pioneers. Meyer indignantly insisted that English and American fighter planes strafed and killed 15,000 people in the meadows next to the Elbe River, where they had fled to escape the burning city. My only recollection of this alleged atrocity was that it was promoted by Paul Joseph Goebbels in 1945 to spur German resistance in a lost cause.

"'What proof do you have of this?' I asked.

"'Proof? The whole world knows this,' Meyer retorted.

"'Americans don't,' I said. 'But do you know that the bombing of Dresden was requested by the Red Army?' Meyer looked at me incredulously. I told him our State Department last year issued a statement explaining the bombing took place because the Soviets wanted to prevent Wehrmacht reinforcements from passing through Dresden to check the forces of Marshal Ivan Konev, then only 60 miles away.

"Hans-Jurgen Meyer changed the subject. 'Why,' he demanded 'were the Americans developing hydrogen bombs for another war?'"

EXCERPTS FROM

THE STRANGE ALLIANCE

BY MAJOR GENERAL JOHN R. DEANE, USA,
U. S. MILITARY MISSION IN MOSCOW IN 1943-1945,
(The Viking Press, New York, 1947), Pages 139-141.

"The Story Of Our Efforts
At Wartime Cooperation
With Russia"

At the Yalta Conference (4-11 February 1945) a formula was worked out whereby the British and American Air Forces would not enter the zone that lay two hundred miles west of the Red Army's front lines without giving the Russians twenty four hours' notice of our intentions. Russian silence was to be taken as consent. The Formula was worked out by Air Chief Marshal Portal, Marshal Khudyakov, General Kuter. (Major General Laurence S. Kuter, now lieutenant general and Commander, Air University, Maxwell Air Force Base, Alabama) We all thought it was an agreement until the last day of the Conference when General Antonov (General A. E. Antonov, Chief of Staff, Red Army

General Staff) said that Russian silence should not be taken as consent but rather as disapproval. The Conference therefore adjourned without agreement having been reached and General Spaatz continued to operate at will, being careful to give the Russians ample notice of operations which might interfere with theirs.

Fortunately for me Major General Edmund W. Hill arrived in Russia in December 1944 as the senior air member of my Mission and commander of Army Air Forces activities in Russia. I was delighted to turn the whole question of air liaison over to him. He worked around the clock, meeting with and sending letters to the General Staff in an effort to keep them fully informed of American air activities on the Russian front. Frequently notice of an American attack would be delayed until after it had been made, and Hill was kept busy explaining such incidents to the Russians. Clashes between our Air Forces occurred with increasing frequency as the Allies converged on the Germans, and Hill had to bear the brunt of Soviet displeasure as if he alone were to blame. Finally, in March 1945, Hill succeeded in obtaining Russian agreement to the arrangement worked out at Yalta, and this was the method of coordination used until the end of the war.

While Soviet requests for American assistance were few, those which were made were invariably granted. In one instance we were requested to bomb the Citadel, the headquarters of the German General Staff about thirty miles south of Berlin. It was thirty four feet underground and heavily constructed of concrete and steel. We had known of its existence for two years before its location became known to the Russians. We had always refrained from attacking it because we felt it was really bomb proof. Upon Soviet request we attacked it heavily, purely as a gesture of collaboration. On another occasion we were asked to launch an attack against Swinemunde, where the Russians reported a huge concentration of German shipping. We launched a particularly violent attack on the harbor through heavy clouds with the help of radar. We could not observe the results and asked the Red Air Force to photograph them for us so that the attack could be repeated if necessary. It took us three weeks to obtain a reply to our request, and then we were not given photographs but simply a report deprecating the value of our attack.

I think the most outstanding lesson that came out of our efforts to coordinate air operations with the Red Army was the effectiveness of positive action as opposed to negotiation when dealing with Soviet officials. Eaker's

(Lieutenant General Ira C. Eaker, USA, Commanding General, Eighth Air Force) arbitrary action in setting his own bomb line in December 1944 was a forceful example of what I mean. We had been attempting for eight months to negotiate an agreement through which we could be of mutual assistance and avoid unfortunate incidents.

On our part it was purely a cooperative effort. It was defeated by the Russians in their search for our hidden motive. They had much more respect for us and acquiesced more readily when we simply informed them that "This is what we are going to do, take it or leave it."

There is merit in considering adherence to similar procedure in the future.

(End of Chapter VIII, "Cooperation of European Air Operations")

UNITED STATES STRATEGIC BOMBING SURVEY

(Originally CONFIDENTIAL, now Unclassified)

REPORT NO. 64-A

"THE IMPACT OF THE ALLIED AIR EFFORT ON GERMAN LOGISTICS"

CHAPTER II, "Transportation"

Final Phase (Page 38)

107. Specific effects of the air attack on transportation during this period are obscured by the chaos accompanying the final collapse of the German military machine. All traffic to and from the Ruhr had been cut off; the water ways of northwestern Germany were virtually idle and the *Reichsbahn* had been forced by lack of communications to abandon the compilation of any statistics. (Reference Note 1 in Index: U.S.S.B.S., Transportation Division Report.) It is worth mentioning that events of previous phases had so reduced the German capacity for resistance that transportation targets as far east as Cottbus and Dresden were attacked in direct support of the Russian ground armies and one air force alone was able to attack, in two days from

relatively low levels, almost one hundred key rail installations in central Germany.

...

ANNEX 4 TO CHAPTER II

The Attack

...

1. b. Overall plans called for attacks on major rail centers and water routes of western Germany with particular emphasis on the isolation of the Ruhr. (Reference Note No. 31: "Review and Operations of the Working Committee (Communications) of the Combined Strategic Target Committee (October 1944 - May 1945).) This basic objective was superseded on several brief occasions in order to implement such special operations as "CLARION" when a large number of small key rail installations were attacked from relatively low altitudes and "VARSITY," a plan under which air was supplied to the 21st Army Group in their crossing of the Rhine. On other occasions, attacks were made at the direct request of Allied ground forces, as at Dresden and Cottbus behind the Russian front, and at Remagen to insure the stability of the United States 1st Army. Finally, with German held territory assuming the shape of an hourglass, transportation attacks were confined to the areas of the "National Redoubt" in south central

Germany and to the alternate escape pocket along the western Baltic coast.

f. The effects of the limited attacks behind the Russian front are summarized in two statements:

(1) General Jodl "Attacks on Dresden eliminated it as a railroad junction completely. But they had no significant effect upon the supply to the east." (Reference Note No. 14: Name, rank, and position of individual: Jodl, General, Chief of Joint General Staff, OKW. USSBS Interview Number 62, 29 June 1945).

(2) Major Joseph Boll, Transport Officer, 4th PZ (Panzer) Army, "Allied bombing of Berlin, Dresden, Chemnitz, Halle, and Cottbus, has dealt a severe blow to whatever west-east or east-west traffic remained . . . ." (Reference Note No. 99: Name, rank, and position of individual: Boll, Josef, Major: Transportation Officer, 4th PZ Army, Report No. 4-1, Mobile Field Interrogation Unit No. 1 21 April 1944 (1945).

UNITED STATES STRATEGIC BOMBING SURVEY

(Second Edition, January 1947)

REPORT NO. 200

THE EFFECTS OF STRATEGIC BOMBING ON GERMAN TRANSPORTATION CRAPTER III, The Design and Weight of an Attack

(Page 15) April 1945

...Heavy attacks in this area followed immediately, while the continued convergence of the Allied and Russian armies toward Dresden began to shape the remaining enemy held territory into two rough triangles, the apex of each joining at that city. About this time it was decided that a fluid ground situation precluded any long term strategic selection of targets, and that henceforth the ground forces would request attacks on a basis of their day-to-day requirements.

REPORT BY THE SUPREME COMMANDER TO THE COMBINED CHIEFS OF STAFF ON THE OPERATIONS IN EUROPE OF THE ALLIED EXPEDITIONARY FORCE, 6 JUNE 1944 TO 8 MAY 1945,
(U.S. Government Printing Office, Washington, D.C., 1946), signed by General of the Army Dwight D. Eisenhower, Supreme Commander, Allied Expeditionary Force.

PLANS FOR THE 1945 CAMPAIGN

Now that the time was approaching for what, we trusted, would be the final blow to Nazi Germany, a closer coordination with the Russian High Command and mutual understanding of our respective plans became essential. Our first liaison with Moscow had been effected late in 1944 when air operations necessitated the establishment of a coordinated bomb line, but little further had been accomplished. The only link between my Headquarters and that of Marshal Stalin was through the medium of the Allied Military Mission in Moscow, and it appeared most difficult to learn of Soviet intentions. Up to the end of 1944 I had received no information on matters affecting the Russian grand strategy, although I had expressed my willingness to afford any such information concerning my own overall plans as the Red Army might desire. At Christmas time, however, following upon a message which I sent to the Combined Chiefs of Staff explaining the difficulty with which I was faced in attempting to evolve plans while still ignorant of the Russian intentions, President Roosevelt secured from Marshal Stalin his agreement to receive our representative in order to discuss the correlation of our respective efforts in the forthcoming spring.

Accordingly, in January, my deputy, Air Chief Marshal Tedder, accompanied by Maj. Gen. Bull (G-3) and Brig. Gen. Betts (G-2), journeyed to Moscow for this purpose. The conference proved conspicuously successful. In the course of a discussion ranging over many aspects of the forthcoming campaigns, Marshal Stalin was acquainted with the nature of our own plans, including the timing. He, in turn, responded with a full explanation of the great four pronged offensive, involving from 150 to 160 divisions, which the Red Army was preparing to launch. He further gave us an assurance that, in the event of the main offensive being halt by bad weather, the Red Army would still conduct local operations which he believed would so pin down the German armies as to permit no major movement of divisions from east to west during the difficult period of the spring thaw. As events showed, the success of this gigantic offensive proved even greater than had been anticipated. In the meantime, fortified by Marshal Stalin assurances, we were able to proceed with our own operational planning. (Page 83)

THE ENVELOPMENT OF THE RUHR AND THE JUNCTION WITH THE RUSSIANS

In central Germany, a route was open to us through the gap in the enemy's line created by the trapping of Army Group B in the Ruhr. An easy advance was thus offered from Kassel, through Erfurt and Leipzig, to Dresden. This would again bring our forces to an important industrial area, the richest still left to the Germans after their loss of the Ruhr and Silesia. There also we should be able to meet the advancing Red Army, and in so doing we should cut in half what remained of Hilter's Reich.

In the south, an axis of advance was available through Nurnberg and Regensburg by the Danube Valley into Austria, where the Russians were already threatening Vienna. A thrust on this axis would also enable us to isolate, and then penetrate, the Redoubt in western Austria into which we now knew the enemy intended eventually to withdraw as many of his forces as possible. The prevention of such a withdrawal was a major objective in any operations which we might execute in the south.(Pages 105-106.)

...

When the central thrust had achieved its object, the principal task was to be an advance to the Baltic and the cleaning out of the whole northern area from Kiel and Lubeck westward by the 21 Army Group. The Ninth Army would, if neccessary, again be used to assist Field Marshal Montgomery in this work. After the requirements for these northern operations had been met, we should be able to direct the 6th Army Group, with perhaps the Third Army, southeastward down the Danube Valley and into the Redoubt.

It will have been observed that in all the possible lines of advance into Germany following the Ruhr encirclement the question arose of effecting a junction with the Russians. In fact, with the approach of our respective forces from east and west, it was now essential that operations on the two fronts should be coordinated, and necessary to learn something of the Russians' intentions in order to know best how to exploit such success as our own plan of campaign might achieve. I therefore informed Marshal Stalin of my general plan to strike first in the center and subsequently to effect a link up with his forces in the

Regensburg-Linz area with a view to neutralizing the Redoubt. Marshal Stalin replied that this scheme coincided entirely with the Russian plans in respect to both the central and southern sectors.(Page 106)

...THE FINAL PHASE.

Prior to the Allied advance across central Germany, evidence had been received that the government was preparing to evacuate Berlin and move southward, ultimately perhaps to Berchtesgaden in the national Redoubt. Some of the departments had already left the city, but the main body now found that, with the Allied link up on the Elbe, it was too late. An impassable barrier had been drawn across the country, and the way to the Redoubt was cut off. In consequence, Hitler and his intimate henchmen stayed on in Berlin.

Although the Redoubt was not, therefore, to be the last seat of the Nazi government, the possibility remained that it would still be the scene of a desperate stand by the fanatical elements of the armies south of the dividing line, together with those which might retreat northward out of Italy. These armies, totaling about 100 nominal divisions, included the bulk of the remaining German armored and SS formations, and up to 30 panzer divisions might conceivably be concentrated behind the mountain barriers. In addition, most of the surviving German jet fighter plane strength was located in the south. The conquest of the Redoubt area thus remained as an important objective of the Allies, despite the collapse of the rest of Germany. In the event of determined resistance, its reduction would constitute a formidable problem, and speed of movement was therefore essential to forestall the enemy's retiring into the area in time to fortify it against our attacks.

Extending some 240 miles in length and 80 miles in depth, the Redoubt comprised the western half of Austria, with small portions of Germany to the north and Italy to the south. It was bounded on the north by the Bavarian Plains, on the south by the Dolomites and Carnic Alps, on the west by the Swiss frontier and the Rhine Valley, and on the east by the Lageneurt Basin and the eastern extremity of the Niedere Tauern. Within it lay Berchtesgaden and Hitler's "Eagle's Nest."

The whole area was extremely mountainous and thus unsuitable for large scale airborne operations while the roads into it followed narrow valleys which could easily be held by determined defenders. The snows and danger of avalanches limited the possibility of any military operations to the summer months between May and October. Although there was no evidence of any completed system of defenses along the natural ramparts, some progress appeared to have been made in this respect along the northern flank. Air reconnaissance also revealed underground constructional activity. It was believed that some subterranean factories had been established in the area, but if any considerable numbers of troops were to be maintained there they would have to rely for their supplies, both of food and ammunition, upon previously accumulated stocks. (Page 112-113)

At the same time that the 21 Army Group concentrated on its principal thrust to Lubeck, a similar advance was to be made in the southern zone down the Danube Valley toward Linz with the Object of effecting a further junction with the Russians. The static situation in the center now permitted the use of the Third Army for this purpose, while the 6th Army Group devoted the whole of its attention to the problem of the Redoubt farther south and west.

Meanwhile XXI and VI Corps had crossed the Danube in the Dillingen area on 22 April, and at Donauworth 2 days later. Pockets of the enemy created south of the river by the converging advances were eliminated, and Augsburg was cleared by XXI Corps on the 28th. Farther west, the Ulm area was reached by VI Corps, which, after a pause occasioned by the moves of the flanking French units, drove on toward the Alpine foothills. The infantry passed through the armor to penetrate the mountains, where the terrain served to slow progress more than did the opposition of the enemy. On 3 May, Innsbruck was taken, and the 103d Division of VI Corps pushed on to the Brenner Pass.

Here, at Vipiteno on the Italian side of the border, a junction was effected during the morning of 4 May with the 88th Division of the U.S. Fifth Army which, after the defeat of the enemy forces in Italy, had struck into the Alps from the south. The danger of an enemy last stand in the Redoubt was finally eliminated, and on the following day the enemy Nineteenth Army capitulated, followed by the whole of Army Group G on 6 May. Among the prisoners taken in the course of the Alpine campaign was the most formidable of my former antagonists, the now retired Field Marshal von Rundstedt. (Pages 115-116.)

THE SURRENDER

Hitler and his close followers determined to carry on the fight. They personally had everything to lose, nothing to gain, by peace now. Amid the disillusionment of their armies and the ruins which daily multiplied in Germany, they deliberately chose to sacrifice the remnants of their country. (Page 118)

Excerpts From *The Army Air Forces in World War II*

Volume III, "Europe: ARGUMENT to V-E Day, January 1944 to May 1945," Chapter XX, "The Climax of Strategic Operations," Published By The USAF Historical Division, Air University, Maxwell Air Force Base, Alabama, (The University of Chicago Press, Chicago, Illinois, 1951).

This Berlin raid and the scheduled attacks on other population centers turned attention briefly again to the question of terror bombing, about which the Nazi propaganda machine was having much to say. The leaders of the AAF had long been on record in opposition to indiscriminate attacks on civilians.

If bombardiers were sometimes less circumspect in this matter, or if Germans found it hard to differentiate between spillage and terror bombing, it nevertheless seemed important during those pre-Hiroshima months not to deviate from the stated policy of attacking legitimate military objectives. But were the current and planned bombardments of German cities which served the eastern front deviations from that policy? General Kuter, who was representing General Arnold at the Yalta conference during Arnold's convalescence from a recent illness, asked Spaatz whether the revised directive of 31 January 1945 authorized indiscriminate attacks on cities. (Message, Kuter to General Spaatz, U13314, 13 Feb. 1945.) From Washington, Lt. Gen. Barney M. Giles cabled his support to Kilter's query, a question which must have seemed inappropriate to direct at Spaatz, who had steadfastly upheld the principle of precision bombing in the face of much pressure. (CM-OUT-37181, Giles to Kuter, 14 Feb. 1945.) He replied that USSTAF was really observing Directive No. 3 and not the revision of 31 January: what had occurred was not a change in priority but a shift of emphasis. The Americans were not bombing cities indiscriminately, but attacking transportation facilities inside cities in missions which the Russians had requested and seemed to appreciate. (Message, Spaatz to Kuter, U14466, 14 Feb. 1945)

While this exchange was taking place, the RAF and Eighth Air Force were carrying out extensive and shattering attacks against railway junctions in Dresden, Cottbus, Magdeburg, and Chemnitz which resulted in widespread ruin to surrounding areas and tragedy to thousands of German civilians. At the height of this campaign a news story widely printed in the United States proclaimed that the senior American air commanders had determined to terrorize the German people into submission. This account, which cleared SHAEF but not USSTAF, grew out of a SHAEF press conference in which an RAF officer described how the air forces planned to bomb large population centers and then attempt to prevent relief supplies from reaching and refugees from leaving them, all part of a general program to bring about the collapse of German economy. (Air Commodore C. M. Grierson's press talk, SHAEF, 16 Feb. 1945) In any event, the news story exaggerated the burden of the press talk and grossly misrepresented the purposes of the AAF. General Arnold was disconcerted about the publicity and by this time was confused in his own mind as to which directive USSTAF was observing. He cabled Spaatz to resolve the matter, implying that he would like to know whether there was any significant distinction between morale bombing and radar attacks on transportation targets in urban areas. Spaatz hastened to reply that he had not departed from the historic American policy in Europe, even in the case of Berlin, and Arnold expressed himself as entirely satisfied with the explanation. (CM-OUT-39730 and 39954, General Arnold to Spaatz, 18, 19 Feb. 1945; CM-IN-18562 and 18745, Spaatz to Arnold, 19 Feb. 1945.)

As the discussion died down, Spaatz straightened out his public relations outlets, Eisenhower heard all about the issue, and AAF Headquarters, aware of the damaging impression the recent publicity had made, took steps to prevent another break. (Ltr., Spaatz to Arnold, 20 Feb. 1945; CM-IN-19100, Anderson to Arnold, 19 Feb. 1945; AC/AS Plans Daily Activity Rpt., 19 Feb. 1945.) (Pages 726-727)

...

The Eighth Air Force devoted two days' effort beginning with 14 February to the central German railway centers which were believed to serve armies opposing the Russians in the east. Three hundred and eleven Fortresses dropped 771 tons on Dresden, 294 dropped 718 tons on Chemnitz, and 340 Liberators unloaded 811 tons on Magdeburg, while small forces struck targets of opportunity in this general area. Dresden, which the heavy bombers had left alone until 1945, had received a terrible bombing from the RAF on the previous night. Smoke was still rising to 15,000 feet by the time the Americans arrived to make their attack by instrument. (General Doolittle at Allied Air Commanders Conference, 15 Feb. 1945.) It was this blow which helped set off the flurry about terror bombing already described. The Secretary of War had to be apprised of Dresden's importance as a transportation center and the Russian request for its neutralization. (Memo for Stimson from Marshall (drafted by Loutzenheiser), 6 Mar. 1945.)

Even the RAF report on the attacks went to unusual length to explain how the city had grown into a great industrial center and was therefore an important target. But if casualties were exceptionally high and damage to residential areas great, it was also evident the city's industrial and transportation establishments had been blotted out. Results at Chemnitz were less decisive, though it too received two extremely severe RAF-AAF bombings within the space of a few hours; its railways were scarcely damaged at al1. (RAF BC Weekly Digest 148; USSTAF Intelligent Summaries 68, p. 15.)

On 15 February over 1,100 Eighth Air Force bombers undertook to bring the oil offensive up to date by attacking reviving refineries and plants. Unusually poor visibility caused most of the bombers to unload on marshalling yards, however, Cottbus caught over 1,000 tons from 435 Fortresses and Dresden received 461 tons from 210 Fortresses, all dropped blind, and results were unassessable because of previous or subsequent raids (pages 731-732).

In order to refine the extensive preparations already made, SHAEF requested the air forces to mount CLARION, a plan of long standing designed to utilize all available Anglo-American air power in a blow at German communications which would affect both economic life and the tactical situation. (page 732)

The direct ancestor of plan CLARION was HURRICANE, the project of the autumn of 1944 to impress the German people with a terrifying display of Allied air might. The plan had met objections based on opposition to terror bombing. On 1 January 1945, General Baker had advised Spaatz against sending heavy bombers to attack transportation targets in small German towns, for there would be many civilian casualties and the German people might be convinced the Americans were barbarians, just as Nazi propaganda charged. Eaker concluded that "you and Bob Lovett are right and we should never allow the history of this war to convict us of throwing the strategic bomber at the man in the street." (Letter, Baker to Spaatz, eyes, 1 Jan. 1945. Mr Robert A. Lovett was Assistant Secretary of War for Air; Mr. Henry L. Stimson was the Secretary of War.) Page 733.

REMARKS ON THE RAF BOMBARDMENT OF DRESDEN

ON THE NIGHT OF 13-14 FEBRUARY 1945, BY MARSHAL OF THE ROYAL AIR FORCE, SIR ARTHUR HARRIS, G.S.B., 0.B.E., A.F.C., FROM *BOMBER OFFENSIVE*, (The MacMillan Company, New York, 1947) CHAPTER IX, PAGE 242

With the German army on the frontiers of Germany we quickly set up GH and Oboe ground stations (radar facilities) close behind many distant objectives when the weather would otherwise have prevented us from finding the target. At the same time the bombers could fly with comparative safety even to targets as distant as Dresden or Chemnitz, which I had not ventured to attack before, because the enemy had lost his early warning system and the whole fighter defence of Germany could therefore generally be outmaneuvered. In February of 1945, with the Russian army threatening the heart of Saxony, I was called upon to attack Dresden; this was considered a target of the first importance for the offensive on the Eastern front. Dresden had by this time become the main centre of communications for the defence of Germany on the southern half of the

Eastern front and it was considered that a heavy air attack would disorganize these communications and also make Dresden useless as a controlling centre for the defence. It was also by far the largest city in Germany, the pre-war population was 630,000, which had been left intact; it had never before been bombed. (Marshal Harris probably meant that the Royal Air Force had not bombed Dresden previously. The Eighth Air Force, USAAF, bombed the city in daylight on six different occasions: 7 October 1944; 16 January, 14 and 15 February, 2 March, 17 April 1945.) As a large centre of war industry it was also of the highest importance. An attack on the night of February 15th-14th by just over 800 aircraft, bombing in two sections in order to get the night fighters dispersed and grounded before the second attack, was almost as overwhelming in its effect as the Battle of Hamburg, though the area of devastation, 1600 acres, was considerably less; there was, it appears, a fire-typhoon, and the effect on German morale, not only in Dresden but in far distant parts of the country, was extremely serious. The Americans carried out two light attacks in daylight on the next two days. I know that the destruction of so large and splendid a city at this late stage of the war was considered unnecessary even by a good many people who admit that our earlier attacks were as fully justified as any other operation of war. Here I will only say that the attack on Dresden was at the time considered a military necessity by much more important people than myself, and that if their judgment was right the same arguments must apply that I have set out in an earlier chapter in which I said what I think about the ethics of bombing as a whole.

Marshal Harris probably meant that the Royal Air Force had not bombed Dresden previously. The Eighth Air Force, USAAF, bombed the city in daylight on six different occasions: 7 October 1944; 16 January, 14 and 15 February, 2 March, 17 April 1945.

EXCERPTS FROM *ROYAL AIR FORCE*
AN "OFFICIALLY COMMISSIONED" HISTORY

By Denis Richards and Hilary St. G. Saunders

(Her Majesty's Stationery Office, London, 1954)

Volume III, "The Fight Is Won," Pages 269-271

The chief feature of the attacks in February, 1945, was two assaults made on the night of 13th/14th February on Dresden. In the first, 244 Lancasters took part, in the second, 529. Altogether 2,659 tons of bombs and incendiaries fell upon the town which was a main centre of communications in the southern half of the Eastern Front. The destruction of these was part of the Anglo-American plan for the support of the Russian advance. The crews of Bomber Command very faithfully fulfilled their task. 'The town', says a pilot who took part in the first attack, 'looked very beautiful ringed with searchlights and the fires in its heart were of different colours. Some were white, others of a pastel shade outlined with trickling orange flames. Whole streets were alight. . . . Yet, as I went over the target, it never struck me as horrible, because of its terrible beauty'.

In the streets that beauty was less apparent. Mrs Riedl, an Englishwoman married to a German, had earlier in the evening reached Dresden, a refugee from Lodz in Poland. .She found shelter in the home of 'a simple German hausfrau', who offered the bed of her soldier son. The sirens presently began to wail, and Mrs. Riedl with her host and hostess and a neighbour carrying a small child, made for the nearest cellar. The electric light failed almost at once, but that was of little consequence for the cellar was very soon lit by the glare of flames from neighbouring buildings. At the end of half an hour the 'all clear' sounded and they went upstairs to find themselves in a world in which 'burning sparks were flying about like snowflakes'. No water was to be had for the mains had been hit, but the house was not on fire though it seemed likely to catch alight at any moment. The three of them were engaged in tearing down curtains and pulling up carpets when once more the sirens sounded. Again they sought the cellar but hardly had they reached it, when thick smoke poured into it and 'we all began to choke. . .' After knocking a series of holes through partition walls they eventually reached the street. Mrs. Riedl crawled through the last hole, dipped the blanket which she carried in a tub half full of dirty water which was standing nearby and flung it, dripping wet, over her head and round her shoulders. These precautions saved her life, and together with about twenty others, who had likewise left the burning cellars, she crouched in the middle of the road where they all remained for seven hours until at long last rain fell and momentarily damped the fires with which they were surrounded. About eight in the morning Mrs. Riedl and her companions began to grope their way out of the town towards the river into which many persons had thrown themselves. Its banks and the open spaces beside them were choked with the bodies of those caught in the open by the second attack.

Later in the day and again on the 15th, American Fortresses added to the devastation. Dresden itself, the 'German Florence' and the loveliest rococo city in Europe, had ceased to exist. The exact number of casualties will never be known, for it was full of refugees at the time. The lowest estimate given by the Russians was 25,000, the highest 32,000; but the Germans themselves, their estimate is based on the numbers treated in improvised hospitals and first aid stations, and on the bodies cremated in the wrecked railway station, put the figure considerably higher.

...

The destruction in Germany was by then on a scale which might have appalled Attila or Genghis Khan. Such devastation as had been inflicted on Dresden left Harris quite unmoved: the town was a centre of government and of ammunition works and a key city in the German transport system. His method of bringing about 'the progressive destruction and dislocation of the German military, industrial and economic systems', had in his view not only been right and proper, but also successful, and had shortened the war. This was in his opinion, the primary consideration. A new directive was however, issued, its object being to drain the enemy's oil resources and to disrupt his communications for good and all. Built-up areas were in future to be attacked only if, by so doing, the Army would be helped in their assault, but area bombing, of which the object was purely to destroy German industry, was to be discontinued. These orders were issued on 6th April and prevailed until the end of the war. Until the night of 2nd/3rd May, when the last attack by night of Bomber Command was carried out, its targets were oil refineries, shipyards and marshalling yards.

TARGET DAMAGE TO DRESDEN, GERMANY ON 14 FEB. 1945

Date /Target: 14 Feb, 1945 Marshalling Yards Effective

Sorties: 316

Method of Sight: British term for radar bombing ("Pathfinder")

Tons of High Explosive and Fragmentation Bombs: 487.7

Tons of Incendiary Bombs: 294.3

Total of Bombs dropped: 782.0

Consolidated statement covering attacks of 7 Oct 1944, 16 Jan and 14 Feb. "K" report also covers attack by RAF Bomber Command on 13/14 Feb. In the main M/Y there is great material damage. Large number of fires burning which involved an engine roundhouse, the Central Goods Depot and many wagons in the heavily loaded yards. Later and further coverage shows that very great damage has been done to the city of Dresden, and within the limits of cover, great areas of devastation are seen. The main areas involved, are the heart of the City, Alstadt, lying on the S. bank of the Elbe, Neustadt, on the N. bank, which is somewhat less severely affected, while a further great area of devastation is seen E. of Alstadt, and N. of the Grosser

Garten, in the district of Johannstadt. Incidents of residential damage, scattered, and in places severe, are seen E. of this area as far as the suburb of Loschwitz. Within the areas mentioned, damage to public and administrative buildings is very severe, and a number of unidentified industrial buildings, some of which were still burning, are also involved. Other damage includes one of the main RR stations and both the Augustus and Carola Bridges are both holed. In addition barracks in the town have been seriously affected.

Coverage unavailable at time of publication for raid of 15 February 1945. Sorties: 210; HE & Frag: 463.1; No I.B.

Source: "K" Report Summarization, Evaluation of Damage to Principal Targets, contained in Eighth Air Force Monthly Summary of Operations, February, 1945, p. 22. (Classification: Formerly RESTRICTED, now UNCLASSIFIED

TESTIMONY BY GERMAN WARTIME MILITARY LEADERS

ON THE EFFECTIVENESS OF STRATEGIC BOMBING BY THE U.S. ARMY AIR FORCES AND ROYAL AIR FORCE WITH PARTICULAR RELATION TO THE DESTRUCTION OF RAIL COMMUNICATIONS.

The following statements were extracted from the illustrated periodical, *IMPACT*, "Strategic Air Victory in Europe," published by the Office of the Assistant Chief of Air Staff, Intelligence, War Department, Washington, D.C., July 1945, Volume III, No. 7, Pages 62-64. (Originally CONFIDENTIAL, now UNCLASSIFIED).

"THE REICH'S EX-LEADERS EXPLAIN WHY THEY WERE BEATEN"

"From the men who tried to run Germany's armies and factories under the impact of Allied air attacks comes some authentic testimony regarding the effectiveness of our air effort. After all, they should know. . . ."

GENERAL FELDMARSCHALL KARL GERD VON RUNDSTEDT, Commander-in-Chief in the West before German surrender; "Three factors defeated us in the West where I was in command. First, the unheard of superiority of your air force, which made all movement in daytime impossible. Second, the lack of motor fuel, oil and gas, so that the Panzers and even the remaining Luftwaffe were unable to move. Third, the systematic destruction of all railway communications so that it was impossible to bring one single railroad train across the Rhine. This made impossible the reshuffling of troops and robbed us of all mobility. Our production was also greatly interfered with by the loss of Silesia and bombardments of Saxony, as well as by the loss of oil reserves in Romania."

GENERAL DER INFANTERIE GEORG THOMAS, military chief of the German Office of Production: "Bombing alone could not have beaten Germany, but without bombing the war would have lasted for years longer."

GENERALEUTNANT ADOLF GALLAND, Chief of Fighters, German Air Force: "In my opinion, it was the Allied bombing of our oil industries that had the greatest effect on the German war potential. Even our supplies for training new airmen were severely curtailed, we had plenty of planes from the autumn of 1944 on, and there were enough pilots up to the end of that year, but lack of petrol didn't permit the expansion of proper training to the air force as a whole.

"In the African campaign and in Sicily and Italy, Allied successes were largely due to Allied air superiority. In my opinion, strategic bombing never forced any great change in German strategy and planning until after the opening of the invasion. Then, disorganization of German communications in the west by strategic bombing caused withdrawal to the German frontier. In the last two months of the war, the crippling of the German transport system brought about the final collapse."

GENERALMAJOR HAAS DETLEF HERHUTH VON ROHDEN, Chief of the Historical Section of the Luftwaffe General Staff (Wehrwissenschaftliche Abteilung 8): "The invasion of Europe would have been impossible without strategic bombing. It was the decisive factor in the long run." (General von Rohden, now dead, was employed by A-2, Headquarters, USAFE, in 1946. Before becoming Chief of the Military Science Historical Section of the Air Force

(Kriegswissenschaftliche Abteilung der Luftwaffe), he had been Chief of the General Staff of the First Air Force (Luftflotte I) on the Eastern front.)

GENERAL DER FLIEGER HANS-GEORG VON SEIDEL, Commander-in-Chief, Luftflotte 10: "I had no first hand experience in the matter, but it is my opinion that without disruption of German communications, the invasion would have been a failure.
"The decisive factor in the German defeat was the disruption of German transport communications by Allied air power."

GENERAL FELDMARSCHALL ALBERT KESSELRING, Commander-in-Chief in the West, succeeding Field Marshal von Rundstedt, and formerly Commander-in-Chief in Italy "Dive bombing and terror attacks on civilians, combined with the heavy bombing, proved our undoing.
"Allied air power was the greatest single reason for the German defeat."

GENERALEUTNANT KARL JACOB VEITH, A.O.C. Flak Training: "The Allied breakthrough would have been utterly impossible without strategic as well as tactical bombing. The destruction of the oil industry and the simultaneous dislocation of the German communication system were decisive."

GENERAL FELDMARSCHALL HUGO SPERRLE, Commander-in-Chief of Luftflotte 3 until the fall of Paris: "Allied bombing was the dominant factor in the success of the invasion. I believe the initial landing could have been made without assistance from the air forces, but the breakthrough that followed would have been impossible without the massive scale of bombing, particularly of the German communications far in the rear.
"Allied air power was the chief factor in Germany's defeat."

GENERAL DER FLIEGER KARL BODENSCHATZ, Chief of "Ministeramt," Air Forces High Command: "The invasion could not have been made without the overwhelming superiority of Allied air power. The German army could not bring up its reserves, as the railways were cut, troops could not be moved by roads in the daylight, and as the nights were short it was very difficult to move troops at all.
"I am very much impressed with the accuracy of American daylight bombing, which really concentrated on military targets, stations, and factories, to the exclusion of others."

REICHSMARSCHALL HERMANN GOERING, Commander-in-Chief of the German Air Force (LUFTWAFFE), made the following remarks during the course of several interrogations:

"I knew first that the Luftwaffe was losing control of the air when the American long range fighters were able to escort the bombers as far as Hanover. It was not long before they were getting to Berlin. We then knew we must develop the jet planes. Our plan for their early development was unsuccessful only because of your bombing attacks."

"Germany could not have been defeated by air power alone, using England as a base, without invasion, because German industry was going underground, and our countermeasures would have kept pace with your bombing. But the point is, that if Germany were attacked in her weakened condition as now, then the air could do it alone. That is, the land invasion meant that so many workers had to be withdrawn from factory Production and even from the Luftwaffe.

"We bombed cities in England instead of concentrating on aircraft and engine factories despite my original intention to attack only military targets and factories, because after the British attacked Hamburg our people were angry and I was ordered to attack indiscriminately.

"Allied precision bombing had a greater effect on the defeat of Germany than area bombing, because destroyed cities could be evacuated but destroyed industry was difficult to replace.

"Allied selection of targets was good, particularly in regard to oil. As soon as we started to repair an oil installation, you always bombed it again before we could produce one ton."

"Before D-Day, 6 June 1944, the Allied attacks in Northern France hurt us the most because we were not able to rebuild in France as quickly as at home. The attacks on marshalling yards were most effective, next came low level attacks on troops, then attacks on bridges. The low flying planes had a terror effect and caused great damage to our communications. Also demoralizing were the umbrella fighters, which after escorting the bombers would swoop down and hit everything, including the jet planes in the process of landing.

"The Allies owe the success of the invasion to the air forces. They prepared the invasion; they made it possible; they carried it through.

"Without the U. S. Air Force the war would still be going on elsewhere, but certainly not on German soil."

EXCERPT ON DRESDEN BOMBING

TAKEN FROM *THE SECOND WORLD WAR, 1939-45,* BY MAJOR-GENERAL J.F.C. FULLER, C.B., C.B.E., D.S.O., (New York, 1949), Page 317. A Celebrated British Military Writer.
(Published By Duell, Sloan, and Pearce, New York, N.Y.)

Thus devastation continued, reaching its climax on 13th February, 1945, when Dresden was destroyed. That night, in two attacks, 800 R.A.F. bombers showered 650,000 incendiary bombs mixed with 8,000 lb. and 4,000 lb. high explosive bombs on the centre of the city. (According to official figures furnished by the British Air Ministry, London, England, to the USAFE Historical Division on 9 November 1954, two waves of "Lancaster" bombers were used, the first wave being composed of 244 bombers and the second, 529, or a total of 773 bombers. The Air Ministry also stated that a total of 2,659 tons of bombs were dropped on Dresden in the attacks on the night of 13-14 February 1945 by the R.A.F.) On the following day the greater part of 1,350 American bombers, escorted by 900 fighters, continued the attack which, on the 15th, was taken up by 1,100 American bombers. (General Fuller is in complete error in quoting the great number of U.S. bombers used in the American daylight attacks made on Dresden on 14 and 15 February 1945. The *Eighth Air Force Target Summary*, "Statistical Summary of All Bomber Attacks, Period 17 August 1942 Thru 8 May 1945," (Page 20) records only 316 sorties flown with 487.7 tons of high explosives and 294.3 tons of incendiary bombs dropped on 14 February 1945, and 211 sorties flown with 465.6 tons of high explosives dropped on 15 February 1945. (From files of USAFE Historical Division) Marshal of the R.A.F. Sir Arthur Harris also states in his Bomber Offensive, page 242, that: "The Americans carried out two light attacks in daylight. . . .") At the time the city was crowded with scores of thousands of refugees fleeing from before the advance of Marshal Koniev's armies. Therefore, the slaughter was appalling: 25,000 people were killed and 30,000 injured; six square miles of the inner town were reduced to ruins; and 27,000 houses and 7,000 public buildings were completely destroyed. (The casualties given by General Fuller may also be subject to question since his source is unknown to the writer. The figures are extremely modest when compared to the much quoted German estimate of 100,000 dead in the 13-14 February 1945 air raid. The higher figure is more readily acceptable by the Germans; however, the writer recalls that in 1946 the Germans were claiming that 300,000 were killed in Dresden. Over a year ago, Chancellor Conrad Adenauer of the German Federal Republic publicly stated that the total civilians killed in Germany during the entire war numbered 500,000. The average German thinks the total was much higher and stubbornly holds this position.

Herr Rumpf in his *Der Hochrote Hahn* gives his German readers the same erroneous figures on American aircraft used against Dresden on 14-15 February 1945 as cited in Major-General Fuller's The Second World War.)

TRANSLATION OF A LEADING EDITORIAL

IN THE *FRANKFURTER ALLGEMEINE ZEITUNG*, MONDAY, APRIL 5, 1954, ENTITLED: "THE ORDERS TO AIR MARSHAL HARRIS."

(Note: A very high ranking military officer recently stated that this article is perhaps the first German attempt to evaluate publicly the Allied strategic air effort. It is included in these Appendices to give the reader the current German attitudes on the Allied bombing of Germany, as contrasted to the cited statements of German military leaders made after the end of the war. The article is interesting also in that it may indicate a new trend in German thinking: that the Second World War was lost by the German Army, but not by the Home Front; a complete reversal of the mythical belief fostered after the First World War, that the German Army was not defeated but "stabbed in the back" by the Home Front. - J. P. Tustin, USAFE Historian).

"*THE ORDERS TO AIR MARSHAL HARRIS*"

"When the war came to an end, something happened to one of the most popular British Generals. Air Marshal (or in

German terminology: General der Flieger) Harris had been in command of air attacks on German cities for several years; until the time of the Normandy landings, he had been the most important man for the British in the conduct of the war in Europe. After the victory, it was to be expected that he was to be highly honored, generally admired, and decorated by both the state and society. Instead, a conspiracy of silence formed about him. People refused to talk about him. He went overseas, and his name appeared to be forgotten. Only last year the British Government remembered this man who had been so powerful during the war, and who had achieved such tremendous deeds. (Whether good or evil will have to be discussed later). The Queen was requested to raise him to the status of nobility. But it appears that this did not solve the problem; the attacks on him persisted. Thus, the official historical war report declared that the attacks on the German civilian population were by no means based on the original plans of Air Marshal Harris; he had merely executed the orders given to him by the government.

An Obedient Soldier

"Whatever excuses may be gathered from this about Air Marshal Harris, namely that he was but an obedient soldier, may perhaps leave a stronger impression in England than in

Germany. We have not yet completely forgotten the interpretations made in Nuremberg by the prosecution, as well as by the judges, according to which no soldier has the right to call upon his duty of obedience if he is given inhumane orders.

But Harris does not require much discussion; he is the less significant figure of air warfare. Historically significant are the horrible errors which were made by the British and American governments during the war. Last week the British Historical Office calmly admitted once more the main error of the British government: it intended to destroy the morale of the civilian population when the German residential areas were set afire, burying thousands of helpless people. (This statement is challenged if Herr Sethe's source is the history of the Royal Air Force cited in this narrative on the bombing of Dresden. If so, his interpretation is incorrect since the history, which was printed earlier this year, makes no such statement. Apparently, Herr Sethe manipulates facts to suit German thinking.)

The Morale Effect

"Once more it is shown, in an irritating fashion, how little the British government knew about the people in a totalitarian state. In such a state there are not only no chances of uprising, but by combining propaganda with compulsion, the forces of the more critical individuals also are utilized for the purposes of the state. Even after the area bombings, the workers went back to their defense factories, and the officials to their offices. The thoughts of every individual were difficult to determine, even then; but they were not important. More important was the fact that they maintained, involuntarily or wholeheartedly, Germany's war machine until finally it collapsed entirely. And the effects of discouragement and fright were probably compensated by indignation and embitterment. The propaganda of Dr. Goebbels had few subjects as rewarding as the air war directed against the civilian population.

It is true that many Germans heard from British broadcasts that it was Hitler who had started the bombing warfare against the civilian population. But even if this had been correct, a fact which has been debated until today, what else could it have meant but that the enemy had dropped to the level of national socialism? How should one continue to believe their contentions that they were fighting for a better world? Under these conditions Germany lost the war, not because the civilian population no longer wanted to continue it, or because it even may have rebelled. It was lost because the Germans in the front lines were beaten in the decisive battles. The destruction of railroad stations and factories contributed to the defeat, but truly not the destruction of residential sections. The armed forces were beaten on the battlefields.

What Has Been Missed

"But they were beaten too late; too late for us and too late for the Anglo-Saxons. Four precious years had elapsed during which the main military efforts of the mighty British Empire were aimed at raising to the tremendous level the military uselessness of war against the civilian population. During this time the Russians fought in the great battles and advanced victoriously, rewinning from the Germans province after province, finally conquering Poland, the Balkan states, and East Germany. When the British and Americans landed in Normandy, the Russians had already penetrated deep into Poland. It was natural that in the subsequent race, the Russians reached Berlin and Prague sooner than the Western Powers. (For the true reason, see *WAR AS I KNEW IT*, by General George S. Patton, Jr., (Houghton Mifflin Company, Boston, 1947), page 330, which states that when General Patton bid farewell to the war correspondents on 9 May 1945 in a final briefing, one correspondent asked: "General, why didn't we take Prague?"

General Patton said, "I can tell you exactly why, because we were ordered not to.")

British experts, as early as 1945, expressed the bitter truth that it would have been possible to execute the Normandy invasion one year earlier. (The Allies were unprepared to invade Europe in 1943. Said General Eisenhower in his *Report By The Supreme Commander*, "America and England, the Western Allies, could not be sufficiently strong to undertake the assault against France until June 1944." (Page viii).) It would have been a year of world historical significance. However, the British experts added, it would have been necessary that the power of the British air force and the defense industry be used for the battle, rather than for the fight against the German hinterland. We may continue that then the Western armies would have penetrated into Germany at a time when the Russians were still being held at the river Don; then the western world would never have had to face the nightmare which now emanates from Berlin, from Dresden, from Prague, from Warsaw or from Budapest. While the western world indulged in the deceptive hope that the war could be won by attacking helpless people, it lost the war. Or who would seriously doubt that the Anglo-Saxons also belong to the losers?

The Palm Of Victory

"The Russians have never delayed their operations by the military folly of wasting their power in a fight against residential areas. It has been said, indeed, that their air force has not been capable of conducting such a war. But it has not been shown that they who created myriads of tanks from virtually nothing did not consider the mass attacks against cities as being important enough to divert a large fraction of their forces to such operations? They certainly have not been more humane than the Western forces. We know how they plundered the country after they conquered it. However, as an old military power, they understood the true nature of war, a concept that the Western powers did not comprehend. It was not simply chance, malice or cunning, and it was neither the delusion of Hitler or Roosevelt's tragic error which gave the Russians power over the Balkan states and Central Europe. According to the military course of the war, it unfortunately was an historical consequence. The Western powers believed they were able to deceive the goddess of victory by having Mr. Harris direct his bombers against residences. Do the Western powers understand by today that this goddess cannot be deceived; do they see why she turned away from them and in 1945 gave the palm of victory to the Russians?

Did The Demons Die?

"This is not being written in order to balance the indictments of atrocities raised against the 'Third Reich.' The disgrace which at that time was heaped upon the German name will not die in a thousand years, and the burning shame in our hearts will not be extinguished in our lifetime. But we must speak openly about the fact that in this century the demons of the blind rage of destruction were unchained not only in our country; elsewhere too they penetrated the shell of civilization; we shudder, learning how thin it had been. It is of no help to be silent. Help can come in every country only from frankness. In this sense, it may represent a ray of hope that a circle of estrangement has formed about 'Bomber-Harris' in Great Britain."

Written by Herr Paul Sethe, Editor

Footnotes

1. *The New York Times*, International Edition, 12 February 1953, page 3, titled: "U.S. Lays Dresden Bombing to Soviet Plea, Spoiling German Reds 'Hate America Line." See Appendix I.

Special Issue of *LIFE* on Germany, 10 May 1954, page 50, titled: "Bombing U.S.S.R. Sought Is Turned Against U.S." See Appendix II.

2. *Der Hochrote Hahn*, by Hans Rumpf, (Darmstadt, Germany, 1952), page 133. In Germany the title, "The Bright-Red Rooster," is symbolic with fire destruction.

3. *Ibid.* Herr Rumpf was a high ranking military fire marshal during the war.

4. At the outbreak of the European war in 1939 the population of Dresden was 625,174. *The Encyclopedia Britannica*, (1954), Volume VII, page 648. The last census, 1946, gave the population of the city and environs as 510,000. Figures furnished by the *Statistisches-bundesamt* (German Federal Republic Statistical Bureau), Wiesbaden Office, 15 November 1954.

5. *Der Tod von Dresden*, (The Death of Dresden), by Axel Rodenberger, (Franz Muller-Rodenberger, Dortmund, Germany, 1953), page 16.

6. In German, "Elbflorenz," or "Florence-on-the-Elbe" river.

7. Literally, "The Murder-Night of Dresden." *Der Hochrote Hahn*, pages 133-134.

8. USSTAF, commanded by General Carl A. Spaatz, USA, comprised: the Eighth Air Force in England, under Lieutenant General Ira. C. Eaker, USA, and later, Lieutenant General James H. Doolittle, USA; the Fifteenth Air Force in Italy (operational control only), under Major General Nathan F. Twining, USA; and the Ninth Air Force on the continent (administrative control only), under Major General Hoyt S. Vandenberg, USA.

9. USSTAF was redesignated as USAFE on 16 August 1945, per Hq. USSTAF General Orders Number 115, 16 August 1945.

10. See remarks on Russian attitudes at Yalta Conference, 4-11 February 1945, by Major General John R. Deane, USA, Chief of the U.S. Military Mission at Moscow. *The Strange Alliance*, (The Viking Press, New York, 1947), Pages 139-141. See Appendix III.

11. *United States Strategic Bombing Survey*, (Europe), Reports Number 64-A and 200, Second Edition, January 1947, Chapter III. See Appendix IV.

12. For a more complete explanation of the National Redoubt and its impact on Allied military planning, see

General of the Army Dwight D. Eisenhower's *Report By The Supreme Commander To The Combined Chiefs of Staff On The Operations In Europe Of The Allied Expeditionary Force, 6 June 1944 to 8 May 1945,* (U.S. Government Printing Office, Washington, D. C., 1946). See Appendix V.

13. *The Second World War*, Volume VI, "Triumph and Tragedy," (Houghton Mifflin Company, Boston, 1953), Chapter XIII, pages 540-541.

14. *Ibid.*, page 460.

15. Earlier, the Eighth Air Force of USSTAF had made two light attacks on Dresden: 7 October 1944 and 16 January 1945. Statistics and source of data cited in next section.

16. Directive Number 3, SHAEF, 12 January 1945, Governing strategic operations of USSTAF and the RAF Bomber Command.

17. The senior members of each of the three services in the United Kingdom were called the Chiefs of Staff and in the United States the Joint Chiefs of Staff. Together they were known as the Combined Chiefs of Staff.

18. *The Army Air Forces In World War II*, "Europe: ARGUMENT to V-E Day, January 1944 to May 1945," (The University of Chicago Press, Chicago, 1951), Volume III, Chapter XX, page 724.

19. *Ibid.*, pages 724-725.

20 *Ibid.* Letter, Major General Frederick L. Anderson, USA, Deputy Commander, USSTAF, to General Carl A. Spaatz, USAF, Commanding General, USSTAF, 2 February 1945, from General Anderson's Journal, ARGONAUT.

21. *Ibid.* Message CM-IN-259, SHAEF to War Department, Washington, D.C., 31 January 1945.

22. U.S.S.B.S., Report Number 64-A. *The Army Air Forces in World War II*, Volume III. January 1944 to May 1945, pages 726-727. See Appendix VI.

23. Air Chief Marshal Harris was appointed Air Commander-in-Chief, Bomber Command, on 22 February 1942, and subsequently, Marshal of the RAF.

24. *Bomber Offensive*, by Sir Arthur T. Harris, Marshal of the RAF, (The MacMillan Company, New York, 1947), page 242. See Appendix VI.

25. Supreme Headquarters Allied Expeditionary Force (SHAEF), London, England, commanded by General of the Army Dwight D. Eisenhower. Before General Eisenhower assumed command of SHAEF the Strategic Air Forces were under control of the Combined Chiefs of Staff; but the Supreme Allied Commander felt that, "since responsibility for the principal effort against Germany fell upon my Headquarters, all the forces to be employed within the

Theater, by land, sea, and air, should be responsible to me and under my direction . . ." ("*Report By The Supreme Commander To the Combined Chiefs Of Staff, Etc.*," previously cited, page 14.

General Eisenhower further explains:

"In the final command set up of the air forces, then, the commanders of the Strategic Air Forces (RAF Bomber Command and the United States Strategic Air Forces) reported to Supreme Headquarters independently as did also Air Chief Marshal Leigh-Mallory, commanding the tactical forces which comprised the Allied Expeditionary Air Force. The effort of the three separate commands was coordinated, under my direction, through the Deputy Supreme Commander, Air Chief Marshal Sir Arthur Arthur W. Tedder." (*Ibid.*, pages 14-15)

26. *Bomber Offensive*, page 242.

27. Dresden comprises two principal parts: Neustadt (New Town), and across the Elbe, Altstadt (Old Town). Greater Dresden embraces the municipal districts of Johannstadt, Striesen, Blasewitz, Friedrichstadt, Lobtau, Plauen, and Strehlen. The principal marshalling yards and main railroad station were in the Old Town, the most beautiful part of the city.

28. *Bomber's Baedeker*, "A Guide to the Economic Importance of German Towns and Cities," Second Edition,

May 1944, Part I, pages 154-161. An official British document published by the Enemy Branch, Foreign Office and Ministry of Economic Warfare, (Landsdowne House, Berkeley Square, London, W. 1). Classification reduced from SECRET to RESTRICTED after the war. Copy formerly in the USAFE Historical Division.

29. *Der Tod von Dresden*, pages 45-47.

30. *Royal Air Force*, an "officially commissioned" history, by Denis Richards and Hilary St. G. Saunders, (Her Majesty's Stationery Office, London, 1954), Volume III, "The. Fight Is Won," pages 269-271. See Appendix VIII.

31. *The Army Air Forces In World War II*, page 731. Remarks by Lt. Gen. James H. Doolittle, Commanding General, Eighth Air Force, at the Allied Air Commanders' Conference, 15 February 1945.

32. "Target Damage To Dresden, Germany, on 14 Feb. 1945." A Consolidated Statement Covering (American) Attacks of 7 October 1944, 16 January, and 14 February; coverage unavailable for air raid of 15 February 1945. From "K" Report Summarization, Evaluation of Damage to Principal Targets, in *Eighth Air Force Monthly Summary of Operations, February 1945*, page 22. Now UNCLASSIFIED; formerly in USAFE Historical Division. See Appendix IX.

33. By comparison, *The Army Air Forces In World War II* states that: "Three hundred and eleven Fortresses dropped 771 tons on Dresden . . . ." (Page 731).

34. "Target Damage To Dresden Germany On 14 Feb. 1945."

35. *Der Tod von Dresden*, pages 10-11. The author is mistaken as to the intensity of the American attack of 14 February. This third attack, made by the Eighth Air Force, was less than one third the weight of the RAF attacks, as noted by the following official statistics: Total tonnage dropped by the RAF on 13-14 February, 2,659; by Eighth Air Force on 14 February, 782. RAF statistics on number of bombers used and number of tons dropped were furnished the USAFE Historical Division by the British Air Ministry, London, on 9 November 1954.

36. *The Army Air Force in WorldWar II*, page 731. Memorandum from General Marshall to the Hon. Henry L. Stimson, Secretary of War, (drafted by Loutzcnhciser), 6 March 1945.

37. *The Army Air Forces In World War II*, page 731. RAF Bomber Command Weekly Digest Number 148, n.d. USSTAF Intelligence Summary Number 69, n.d., page 18.

38. Missing from text.

39. *Der Tod von Dresden*, *Der Hochrote Hahn*, passim.

40. *The Army Air Forces in World War II*, page 731. RAF Bomber Command Weekly Digest Number 148, n.d.

41. Albert Speer was sentenced by the Nuremberg Tribunal on 1 October 1946 to twenty years imprisonment, which he is now serving at Spandau prison in Berlin.

42. Excerpt from "Comments On The Effects Of The Allied Bombing Of The Reich," by Albert Speer, Former Reich Minister for Armaments and War, Production, in Unclassified magazine, *DEFEAT*, published by Headquarters, Army Air Forces, Washington, D.C., January 1946, page 19.

43. U.S.S.B.S. Interview Number 62, 29 June 1945, with Colonel General Alfred Gustav Jodi, Chief of the Joint General Staff, O.K.W. (Oberkommando der Wehrmacht), Annex 4 to Chapter II, Report Number 64-A. Appendix IV.

44. RAF Bomber Command made four attacks on Hamburg in July and August 1943 with 2,630 bombers dropping 8,621 tons of bombs. USSTAF also carried out a daylight attack with 68 bombers; tonnage of bombs unknown. Six hundred acres were burned out; the general commanding defense reported to Hitler that "The damage was gigantic." The known dead numbered 41,800 persons, 37,439 injured (many died), and "some thousands more missing." *Royal Air*

Force, Volume III, "The Fight Is Won," Chapter I, pages 5-9.
45. *Der Tod von Dresden*, page 150.
46. *Der Deutsche Generalstab*, (The German General Staff), by German General Walter Gorlitz, (Verlag der Frankfurter Hefte, Frankfurt am Main, 1953), page 494.
47. *The Last Days Of Hitler*, by H. R. Trevor-Roper, (The MacMillan Company, New York, 1947), Chapter III, page 79.
48. *Der Tod von Dresden*, pages 168-169.
49. *Ibid.*, page 169.
50. Magazine *LIFE*, "Germany, A Giant Awakened," 10 May 1954, page 50. See Appendix II.
51. *Royal Air Force*, Volume III, page 270.
52. *Der Hochrote Hahn*, page 134; *Der Deutsche Generalstab*, page 494.
53. *Bomber Offensive*, page 242. (Underscoring in red by historian). Marshal Harris, (allegedly called "Butcher Harris" by the Germans), cites in his book that the British Government issued a "White Paper" after the First World War (1914-1918) which estimated that the British blockade of Germany caused nearly 800,000 deaths, mainly women, children, and old people, due to food scarcity on the home front. In his defense, Marshal Harris states: "Whenever the

fact that our aircraft occasionally killed women and children is cast in my teeth I always produce this example of the blockade, although there are endless others to be got from the wars of the past." Marshal Harris also states that "the Americans have put the number of deaths from bombing at 305,000" in the last war, with no estimate of how many were women and children. *Bomber Offensive*, pages 176-177. These fatality figures were obtained from the *U. S. Strategic Bombing Survey* which could not cover the Soviet Zone of Germany. In a news report of approximately a year ago, Chancellor Dr. Konrad Adenauer of the Federal German Republic put the estimated total number of German civilians killed by bombing at 500,000.

54. "Testimony By German Wartime Military Leaders On The Effectiveness Of Strategic Bombing By The U. S. Army Air Forces and Royal Air Force, With Particular Relation To The Destruction Of Rail Communications," from *IMPACT*, published by the Office of the Assistant Chief of Air Staff, Intelligence, War Department, Washington, D. C., July 1945, Volume III, Number 7, Pages 62-64. See Appendix X.

55. *Prowling Russians Forbidden Zone*, by Werner Knop, (Alfred A. Knopf, New York, 1949), pages 93-95. Mr. Knopf's family had emigrated from Germany to the U. S.

The Soviet reference to the tactical use of their air fleets is correct: they had no strategic bomber air force whatsoever. The author is right regarding the destruction of old castles and beautiful palaces in the Soviet Zone after the war. Originally, an order was issued directing the blowing up of all century-old architectural structures and monumental buildings which, to the Russians, were symbolic of "capitalistic decadence." Fortunately this order was never fully carried out, presumably to coddle sympathy from East Germans in the new Soviet hate propaganda directed against the U. S.

56. Brigadier Desmond Young's *ROMMEL*, (London, 1954), Chapter X, page 205, states that Vice Admiral Ruge, who commanded the German naval forces in Italy, reported the following conversation with Field Marshal Erwin Rommel in 1944:

> On June llth we talked for about two hours. I said that in my opinion Hitler ought to resign and open the road to peace. As an alternative, I said that he ought to commit suicide. Rommel replied:
>
> "I know that man. He will neither resign nor kill himself. He will fight, without the least

> regard for the German people, until there isn't a house left standing in Germany."

Although Hitler did kill himself rather than surrender (according to documented testimony), his expressed policy of destruction is clear from these words he spoke to Albert Speer in March 1945:

> If the war is to be lost, the nation also will perish. This fate is inevitable. There is no need to consider the basis even of a most primitive existence any longer. On the contrary, it is better to destroy even that, and to destroy it ourselves. The nation has proved itself weak, and the future belongs solely to the stronger Eastern nation. Besides, those who remain after the battle are of little value; for the good have fallen.

On such inhuman overtones, Hitler, that day, issued new orders of destruction: the fight was to be continued, "without consideration of the German people." Said Speer of Hitler: "He was deliberately attempting to let the people perish with himself. He no longer knew any moral boundaries; a man to whom the end of his own life meant the end of everything." *The Last Days Of Hitler*, Chapter III, pages 78, 81, 82.

Made in the USA
Monee, IL
01 February 2020

21180313R00052